Mesmerizing

Moments that life is made of

Pratiksha Hemrajani

BookLeaf Publishing

India | USA | UK

I am forever thankful to my parents for everything. I also wanted to say thank you to all those who love me unconditionally. I am who I am because of you.

Thank you to my dear readers. I am utterly thankful to each one of you.

Acknowledgment

I would like to thank BookLeaf for a wonderful experience.

Preface

I have thoroughly enjoyed writing this book.
I am a perfume creator by profession and a dreamer at heart.
When I write, time and space cease to exist.
This is for all my readers who like escapism :)

With love,
Pratiksha Hemrajani

Gift

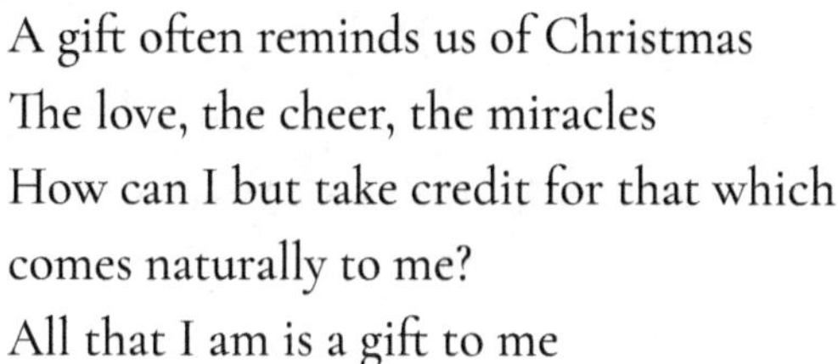

A gift often reminds us of Christmas
The love, the cheer, the miracles
How can I but take credit for that which
comes naturally to me?
All that I am is a gift to me

la la la la la la la la la la la la

Everyone says that I am an amazing person
I just say I don't know how all the pieces add
up
All I can say is that I do what I can and I hope
to do the same until my very last breath
And I hope that I do it with my love by my
side

Rose

I love my softness
I love my velvet touch
I love my fragrance that touches your heart
and makes your eyes light up
I know that I become your happy memory
I am so grateful that you love me so much
I am stardust after all
And so are you

Love,
Rose

Dream

Who are we if not what we dream
Bombay is a city of dreams and rightly so
The sparkle in the eye
The twirl in our step
The walk of success
The gaze of mesmerism
Oh how beautiful is the dream

The promised castle

She just gazes at the vast ocean, the vast open
space
Immersed in the moment
Oh the sweetness she feels
Oh the sweetness she feels

She takes a walk on a path of pebbles under
water
Only enough water that reaches up to her
ankles
A road that leads her to the promised castle
She walks and walks and right in the middle
of the ocean
This path leads her to the promised castle
Oh the sweetness she feels
Oh the sweetness she feels

Illusion

Uncertainty may feel like humility, but that's an illusion

Obedience may feel like respect, but that's an illusion

Anger may feel like arrogance, but that's an illusion

Pain may feel like effort, but that's an illusion

Darkness may feel like light, but that's an illusion

Why

Why did that fun have to end?
Why did it all have to be a lie?
Why did that version of me have to die?
Maybe just to be reborn again to tell me that
she can never die.

A glass becomes a cup

You can see my glitter but you cannot see
through me
I am cozy and mysterious
Life unfolds magically
As I let it happen
A glass becomes a cup
As I let it happen

No need to prove anything
No need to overshare
Life becomes more relaxed
As I let it happen
A glass becomes a cup
As I let it happen

The smell of love

The smell of love is deep in my being
I smelt it for the first time when I was
studying in France
A strip of L'instant magic by Guerlain
I dipped a strip in the tiny glass bottle
And the smell of love became a bubble
around me
A big cotton ball, soft and thick
Bergamot on top, roses and lilies in the heart,
musk and a touch of vanilla in the base
I used to dip a strip and keep it with me while
sleeping
A smell that will stay with me even after I am
long gone

The smell of time

What is the smell of time, of eternity?
Seems like l'air du temps by Nina Ricci and
forever and ever by Dior have the answer
A white carnation that smells like pure milky
jasmine with a touch of dense, rich clove that
screams royal heritage is the smell of time...
Don't ask me why I don't know why but I do
know that if time has a smell, it is a white
carnation
What else can time be if not pure and royal at
the same time?

Be yourself

I don't want to tell you what to do
But if you want me to tell you something, I'll
say be yourself
Don't try to be happy
Don't try to be thankful
Don't try to fake it till you make it
Just be yourself and you will be okay

The color pink

I am the color pink
I am beyond comprehension
I am soft and mesmerizing
I am like a hug
I make your heart melt
All eyes stop and stare
I can be a phone and a frock
I see no boundaries
I have no judgment
I am the color pink
I am here to love you

Christmas in Paris

Fairy lights and Christmas carols
A bite of almond ganache in the stollen
Christmas trees with the promise of magic
How amazing is Christmas

Spiced wine in the air of Christmas
Reminds us that it's time for magic
Happy endings and fairy tales are real
How amazing is Christmas

Thank you

Some people like to give give give to me
Those who have given given and given to me
You make me speechless
I don't know how to thank you enough
I am who I am because of you

You make me calm
You make me smile
You make me reach for the moon and the
stars
You mean the world to me
I am who I am because of you

I like to give give give to you too
Only because I love you too

Think of you

I see my feet and I think of you
I see my fingers and I think of you
I see my eyes and I see you there
I feel the touch of your finger on my arm
Your eyes gazing through me
Take me anywhere I don't care
As long as it's you and me together, I don't
really care

Garden of Eden is both on Earth and in the
sky above
Two hearts that beat as one
My heart and soul belong to you
Everything reminds me of you

A full cup

When I am happy, I spread so much
happiness
Clearly, the world needs me to be happy
Everywhere I go, I sparkle some love
My cup overfloweth
And together
All our cups overfloweth

The gaze of an antelope

In that moment
Only that moment existed
The gaze of an antelope
As he playfully flapped his ears

He looked into my eyes
And tried to talk to me
I don't think I understood what he said
But happiness was all that was left

The gateway

Use your grey matter
It's who you are
It is easy to run
But it's not so much fun
Use your grey matter
You will be surprised at what you see
Moonlight and sunshine at your feet

The stars

The stars in my eyes seem to appear out of
nowhere
when I think of you
I feel them fill all that I am as if nothing else
exists
It's us forever
As if us was me, is me, and will be me forever

The stars above go above and beyond
The dazzle that you think I am
Every time I look at a star, it reminds me of
that
Not a day goes by that I don't think of you

I believe in love
I believe in fairy tales
I believe in the magic that I see

Bedtime

In the dim lights
In my blanket
A cozy bubble
My comfort zone
This is where I belong

It smells cool and round
It feels like sitting by the fireplace in my
house while it snows outside

It smells like cool breeze on my face
The top note is icy ozone with a creamy heart
and a woody oak base

Serenity

After quite some time
I saw you again
The serenity I've always known
I saw you again
The serenity outside made me meet you again
The wave and the ocean are one again

Mummy and papa

Dear mummy and papa
I love you so much
How are you so wonderful
Always showing me the way
You make me feel like a princess
Being in your embrace makes me feel like I
have the whole world at my feet
Like a tigress and tiger, you protect your cub
And like magic, you see through me
I love you, mummy and papa
And I love to see you happy

About the Author

Pratiksha Hemrajani specializes in perfumes. She obtained her double master's degree from Groupe ISIPCA, European Fragrance and Cosmetic Masters from Versailles, France and Masters in Business Management from Padova, Italy. She has created perfumes for renowned brands globally and across industries and has also been featured on Band Baajaa Bride on NDTV Good Times.

She loves writing and wanted to share something for those who like to be transported while reading.